Snuggle Up

8 Lap Quilts to
Warm Your Home

Beth Merrill Kovich and

Retta Warehime

Martingale™
& COMPANY

Snuggle Up: 8 Lap Quilts to Warm Your Home
© 2002 by Beth Merrill Kovich and Retta Warehime

That Patchwork Place® is an imprint of
Martingale & Company™.

Martingale & Company
20205 144th Avenue NE
Woodinville, WA 98072-8478 USA
www.martingale-pub.com

CREDITS

President • *Nancy J. Martin*
CEO • *Daniel J. Martin*
Publisher • *Jane Hamada*
Editorial Director • *Mary V. Green*
Managing Editor • *Tina Cook*
Technical Editor • *Dawn Anderson*
Copy Editor • *Ellen Balstad*
Design Director • *Stan Green*
Illustrator • *Robin Strobel*
Cover and Text Designer • *Trina Stahl*
Photographer • *Brent Kane*

Printed in China
07 06 05 04 03   8 7 6 5 4 3

MISSION STATEMENT

We are dedicated to providing quality products and service by working together to inspire creativity and to enrich the lives we touch.

Library of Congress Cataloging-in-Publication Data

Kovich, Beth Merrill
  Snuggle up: 8 lap quilts to warm your home / Beth Merrill Kovich, Retta Warehime.
    p. cm.
    ISBN 1-56477-464-3
    1. Quilting—Patterns. 2. Patchwork—Patterns.
I. Warehime, Retta. II. Title.
    TT835 .K684 2002
    746.46'041—dc21

                               2002007827

Dedication

To Pam Clarke, for her extraordinary effort in our behalf and for her commitment to the evolving art of custom long-arm machine quilting.

Acknowledgments

FROM BETH

My entire family deserves the biggest thank-you for this effort. They were nice to me even when I had thread stuck to my clothes, and they seemed to know just when I needed a glass of water or a great big hug. They also didn't seem to miss the dining room table too much when it was buried in fabric and anchored with a sewing machine. Thanks, especially, to Tom.

I feel very fortunate to have had the chance to work with Retta Warehime. She is talented, fun, and a really nice person too. I am grateful for the experience. Thank you!

Big thanks go to Pam Clarke and Frankie Schmitt for the machine quilting services they provided. Thank goodness they are not intimidated by Federal Express packages or late-night pick ups in pajamas. They do it all with a smile.

Martingale & Company—from the concept forward, the great team there has made publishing our book a joy. No one truly knows how much of the work you do. Thanks, also, for giving Retta and me the chance to work together.

I would personally like to thank my good quilting buddies, anonymous as always, for their support behind the scenes of this project. You know who you are—from consulting on sketches to fabric shopping, and from the Federal Express counter to binding, you've been with me every step of the way. These projects are a tribute to the wonderful fellowship I've found in quilting. Let me know when it's my turn to press for you.

FROM RETTA

Thank you to all my quilting friends.

I want to thank Pam Clarke for all her help in meeting my deadlines for this book, as well as for all the other projects she has helped me with in the past two years. Pam, you make it easier for me to sleep nights!

Beth Kovich—what a joy it was to work with you! This was the easy way to make a friend for life. Congratulations on your new baby.

Martingale & Company—wow!

Contents

Introduction

$\mathcal{T}$HE PURPOSE OF this book is to guide you in creating beautiful, useful quilts for the social rooms in your home. By having two designers rather than one develop the quilt plans for you, we hope you will find a greater variety of quilts to choose from and that there will be at least one quilt that you'll be anxious to begin immediately. We encourage you to add your own personal touch. All of the quilts are simple to make and have straightforward instructions. We suggest that you first read through "Quiltmaking Essentials" (page 48) to familiarize yourself with the techniques we've used in the projects. It really does cover the essentials, and we find ourselves referring to it often. Most of all, we believe in speedy sewing and having fun, so turn on some music or an audiobook and get started!

What Is a Snuggle-Up Quilt?

Well, a snuggle-up quilt can be whichever quilt you wrap up in on a rainy day with a good book, or it can be the quilt you're about to make with the help of this book. For us, snuggle-up quilts are meant to be used by our families, friends, and even ourselves. These quilts are destined to be the real workhorses in your collection, loved by every member of your household and washed repeatedly. These quilts will probably sneak their way into a lot of family photos over the years. Your kids may even try to steal them when they leave home or when they come to visit. The quilts are all big enough to cuddle up under (some are even made for two!), but not so big that you'll never get them finished. They are plaid, flannel, patriotic, or floral (to name a few). They might live on an easy chair in your bedroom, grace the settee in your living room, or be everybody's first choice in the family room, but these quilts will be part of your family's everyday life. What gathering room in your house doesn't need a quilt?

When you're ready to begin, we suggest that you select a design first and then choose fabric colors that complement your home, your furnishings, and your sense of style. The projects in this book provide you with examples of color palettes and designs that work well in the homes we frequent. Whatever combination you choose, the best result will be the deep satisfaction that comes from having created something beautiful and useful for a special place in your home. The fact that everyone will claim your snuggle-up quilt as their own is something we consider to be the highest compliment a quilter can receive from family and friends.

Opening Day

This rich-color-palette quilt is perfect for any of the men in your life. Based on a traditional block called Railroad Crossing, it will add a special touch to your family room, den, or even a dorm room. Big blocks, easy piecing, and a carefully planned layout result in a dramatic overall effect and a quilt perfect for all skill levels. This quilt was custom-made for my husband, Tom. He requested that it be very long so that he could tuck it under his feet on the couch, and be big enough for two. You'll notice that the finished dimensions are almost the same as a regular queen-size quilt, but don't be frightened—this quilt works up quickly. —BK

Materials

All yardages are based on 42"-wide fabrics.

- ✧ 3½ yds. main black plaid for blocks, outer border, and binding
- ✧ 1¼ yds. green miniature check for blocks and middle border
- ✧ 1⅜ yds. off-white print for blocks
- ✧ 1 yd. black-and-red print for blocks and inner border
- ✧ ¾ yd. dark red floral for blocks
- ✧ ¾ yd. bright red plaid for blocks
- ✧ ½ yd. black star print for blocks
- ✧ ½ yd. light green leaf print for blocks
- ✧ ½ yd. medium green print for blocks
- ✧ ½ yd. medium green geometric print for blocks
- ✧ 7⅜ yds. fabric for backing
- ✧ 86" x 98" piece of batting

Block Assembly

EACH RAILROAD Crossing block consists of 2 matching green and black half-square triangles and 2 matching red and off-white Four Patch blocks. The red Four Patch blocks are made from strip sets.

1. Join each of the red strips with an off-white strip to make strip sets A and B as shown. Press seams toward the red fabric. From each of the strip sets, cut 60 segments, 3½" wide.

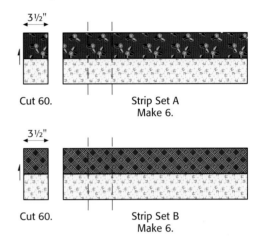

Cut 60.   Strip Set A Make 6.

Cut 60.   Strip Set B Make 6.

Cutting

Fabric	Used For	Number to Cut	Size to Cut	Second Cut
Dark red floral	Blocks	6 strips	3½" x 42"	
Bright red plaid	Blocks	6 strips	3½" x 42"	
Off-white print	Blocks	12 strips	3½" x 42"	
Black star print	Blocks	2 strips	6⅞" x 42"	7 squares, 6⅞" x 6⅞" ◻
Black-and-red print	Blocks	2 strips	6⅞" x 42"	7 squares, 6⅞" x 6⅞" ◻
	Inner border	7 strips	1¾" x 42"	
Main black plaid	Blocks	4 strips	6⅞" x 42"	16 squares, 6⅞" x 6⅞" ◻
	Outer border	9 strips	6½" x 42"	
	Binding	9 strips	2½" x 42"	
Light green leaf print	Blocks	2 strips	6⅞" x 42"	7 squares, 6⅞" x 6⅞" ◻
Medium green geometric print	Blocks	2 strips	6⅞" x 42"	7 squares, 6⅞" x 6⅞" ◻
Green miniature check	Blocks	2 strips	6⅞" x 42"	7 squares, 6⅞" x 6⅞" ◻
	Middle border	8 strips	3" x 42"	
Medium green print	Blocks	2 strips	6⅞" x 42"	9 squares, 6⅞" x 6⅞" ◻

◻ Cut squares once diagonally.

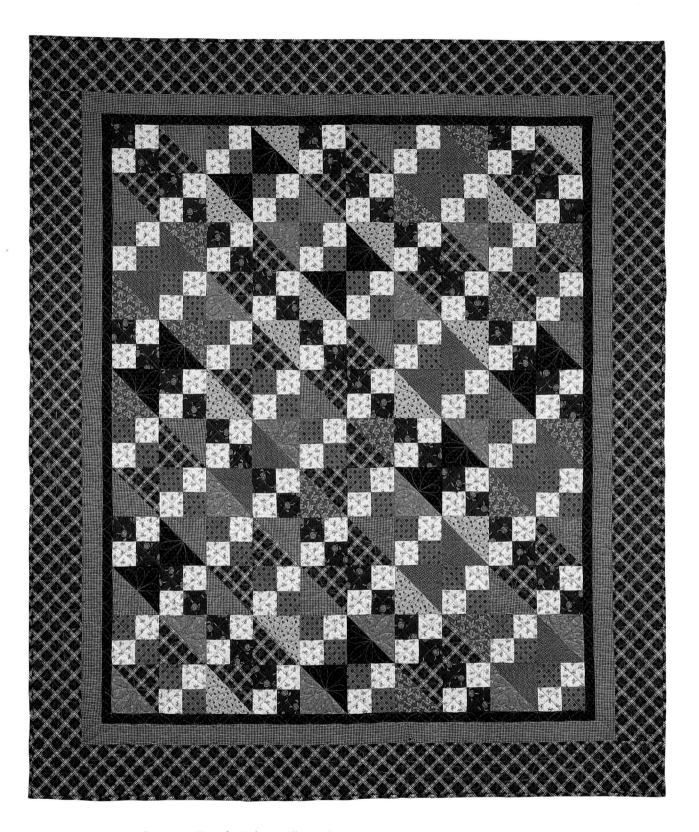

OPENING DAY *by Beth Merrill Kovich, 80" x 92". Machine quilted by Pam Clarke.*
Finished Block Size: 12"; Number of Blocks: 30

2. Join 2 matching segments from step 1 to make Four Patch blocks as shown.

Make 30.

Make 30.

3. Join a pair of matching black triangles to a pair of matching green triangles, along the long edges. Press seams toward black fabric. Trim off points.

Make 60
(30 matching pairs).

4. Join a matching pair of half-square-triangle units from step 3 and a matching pair of Four Patch blocks as shown to make a Railroad Crossing block. Make 30 total.

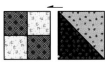
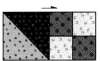 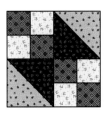

Make 30.

Assembly and Finishing

1. Arrange the blocks into 6 rows of 5 blocks each, alternating dark red and bright red blocks as shown. Sew the blocks into horizontal rows.

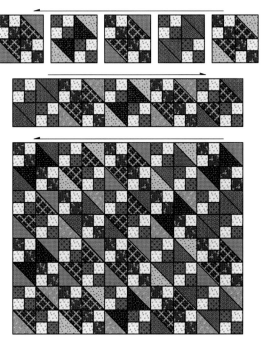

Quilt Assembly Diagram

2. Join the rows together.

3. Referring to "Butted-Corner Borders" on page 55, measure and trim the inner border strips and sew them to the side edges of the quilt top first, and then the top and bottom edges. Repeat for the middle border and the outer border strips.

4. Piece and trim the backing fabric so it is approximately 6" larger than your quilt top.

5. Layer the quilt top with the batting and backing; baste. Quilt as desired.

6. Trim the batting and backing fabric so their edges are even with the quilt-top edges. Bind the edges and add a label.

Crossing Paths

The design for "Crossing Paths" is one I had in my head for a long time. The colors and mix of flannels make this one of my favorite quilts, so I decided to keep it for myself. I chose to accent the warm-colored light background fabric with a wonderful collection of cozy darks and rich brights. By using the same light fabric for the border of this quilt, the pieced design appears to float. The large light areas of the design are the perfect place to showcase a fancy quilting motif.—RW

Materials

All yardages are based on 42"-wide fabrics, unless otherwise stated. Choose a variety of dark, medium, and light fabrics.

- ✧ 3 yds. tan-and-gold check for block backgrounds and outer border
- ✧ 1½ yds. black print for blocks and inner border
- ✧ 3 fat quarters of assorted greens for blocks
- ✧ 3 fat quarters of assorted blues for blocks
- ✧ 3 fat quarters of assorted reds for blocks
- ✧ 3 fat quarters of assorted golds for blocks
- ✧ 5 yds. fabric for backing
- ✧ ⅝ yd. dark print for binding
- ✧ 63" x 87" piece of batting

Block Assembly

1. Join green, blue, red, and gold strips randomly to make 10 strip sets with 2 strips each. From the strip sets, cut 96 segments, 2" wide.

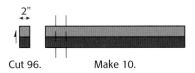

Cut 96.   Make 10.

2. Randomly join pairs of segments as shown to make 48 of unit A. Make sure seams that need to match are pressed in opposite directions.

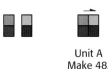

Unit A
Make 48.

3. Join green, blue, red, and gold strips randomly to make 10 strip sets with 4 strips each. From the strip sets, cut 96 segments, 2" wide.

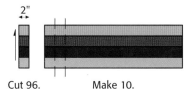

Cut 96.   Make 10.

4. Randomly join 4 segments from step 3 as shown to make 24 of unit B. Make sure seams that need to match are pressed in opposite directions.

Unit B
Make 24.

5. Using a ruler and a light-colored pencil, draw a diagonal line from corner to corner on the back of the black print squares. Position 1 square on

Cutting

Fabric	Used For	Number to Cut	Size to Cut	Second Cut
Each green	Blocks	6 strips	2" x 20"	
Each blue	Blocks	6 strips	2" x 20"	
Each red	Blocks	6 strips	2" x 20"	
Each gold	Blocks	6 strips	2" x 20"	
Black print	Triangles	9 strips	3½" x 42"	96 squares, 3½" x 3½"
	Inner border	7 strips	2" x 42"	
Tan-and-gold check	Block backgrounds	8 strips	3½" x 42"	48 rectangles, 3½" x 6½"
		12 strips	3½" x 42"	48 rectangles, 3½" x 9½"
	Outer border	7 strips	3½" x 42"	
Dark print	Binding	7 strips	2½" x 42"	

CROSSING PATHS *by Retta Warehime, 57½" x 81½". Quilted by Pam Clarke.*
Finished Block Size: 12"; Number of Blocks: 24

top of a 3½" x 6½" background rectangle, right sides together, matching left edges as shown. Stitch on the marked line. Trim seam ¼" from the stitching; press seam toward the black fabric to make unit C. Make 48 total.

Unit C
Make 48.

6. Position 1 black square on top of a 3½" x 9½" background rectangle, right sides together, matching left edges as shown. The diagonal line should run in the opposite direction of the line used for unit C. Stitch on the marked line. Trim seam ¼" from the stitching; press seam toward the black fabric to make unit D. Make 48 total.

Unit D
Make 48.

7. Join unit C pieces to opposite sides of unit B.

 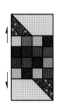

Make 24.

8. Join each unit A piece to a unit D piece as shown.

Make 48.

9. Join unit A-D pieces to opposite sides of unit B-C pieces as shown to complete a block.

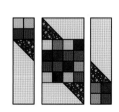 

Make 24.

Assembly and Finishing

1. Arrange the blocks into 6 rows of 4 blocks each as shown. Sew the blocks together in horizontal rows.

Quilt Assembly Diagram

2. Join the rows together.

3. Referring to "Butted-Corner Borders" on page 55, measure and trim the inner border strips and sew them to the side edges of the quilt top first, and then to the top and bottom edges. Repeat for the outer border strips.

4. Piece and trim the backing fabric so it is approximately 6" larger than the quilt top.

5. Layer the quilt top with the batting and backing; baste. Quilt as desired.

6. Trim the batting and backing so their edges are even with the quilt-top edges. Bind the quilt and add a label.

Americana Stars

The tragic events of September 11, 2001, and my love for Americana were the inspiration for this quilt. The striking combination of crisp red, white, and blue is a perennial favorite among quilters. Give this lovely quilt a place of honor in your home, whether it be on the sofa, in the den, or on the wall of your entry. This quilt would also make a wonderful gift for any dads or grads on your gift list. My friend Mary-Lynn Konyu will enjoy this quilt in her Americana room. —RW

Materials

All yardages are based on 42"-wide fabric.

- ✧ 1⅔ yds. white for background
- ✧ 1½ yds. dark blue for sashing squares, blocks, and border
- ✧ 1¼ yds. red for star points, sashing strips, and border squares
- ✧ ⅜ yd. medium blue for block centers
- ✧ 3⅞ yds. fabric for backing
- ✧ ½ yd. red print for binding
- ✧ 54" x 67" piece of batting

Block Assembly

1. Using a ruler and a pencil, draw a diagonal line from corner to corner on the back of the 2⅞" background squares. Position a background square on top of a dark blue square, right sides together. Stitch ¼" from each side of the marked line. Cut on the marked line; press seams toward the background fabric. Trim off points. Make 144 half-square-triangle units.

Make 144.

2. Join 3 half-square-triangle units and a 2½" background square as shown to make unit A.

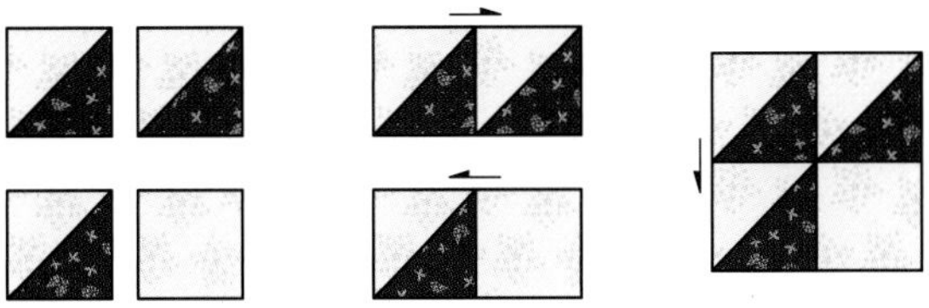

Unit A
Make 48.

3. Using a ruler and a pencil, draw a diagonal line from corner to corner on the back of the 2½" red squares. Position a red square on top of a 4½" background square, right sides together. Align the lower left corners as shown. Stitch on the marked line. Trim seam ¼" from the stitching. Press seam toward the red fabric. Repeat on the lower right corner of the background square to make unit B.

Unit B
Make 48.

Cutting

Fabric	Used For	Number to Cut	Size to Cut	Second Cut
White	Background	6 strips	2⅞" x 42"	72 squares, 2⅞" x 2⅞"
		3 strips	2½" x 42"	48 squares, 2½" x 2½"
		6 strips	4½" x 42"	48 squares, 4½" x 4½"
Dark blue	Sashing squares	1 strip	1½" x 42"	20 squares, 1½" x 1½"
	Blocks	6 strips	2⅞" x 42"	72 squares, 2⅞" x 2⅞"
	Border	6 strips	4½" x 42"	
Red	Star points	6 strips	2½" x 42"	96 squares, 2½" x 2½"
	Sashing strips	11 strips	1½" x 42"	31 strips, 1½" x 12½"
	Border squares	1 strip	4½" x 42"	4 squares, 4½" x 4½"
Medium blue	Block centers	2 strips	4½" x 42"	12 squares, 4½" x 4½"
Red print	Binding	6 strips	2½" x 42"	

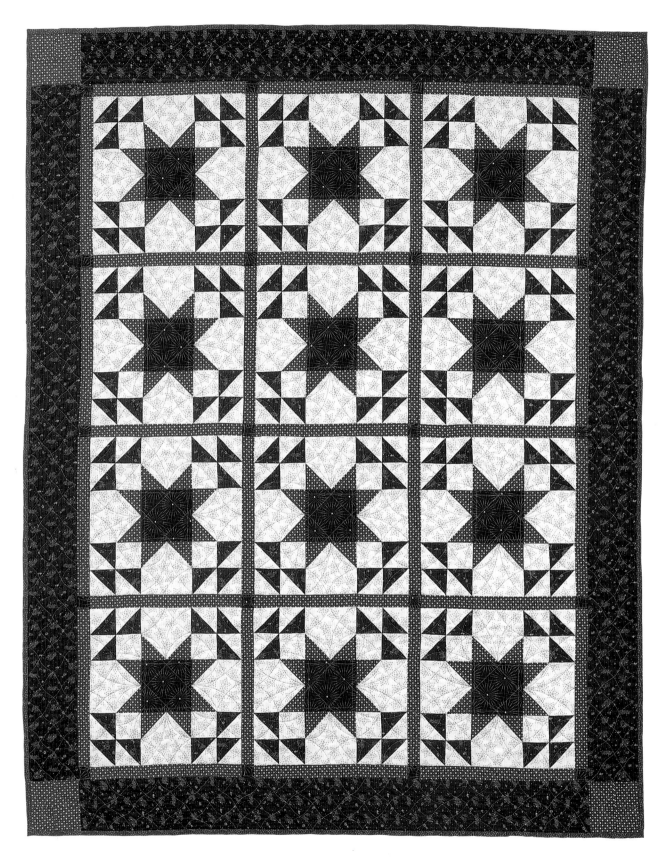

AMERICANA STARS *by Retta Warehime, 48½" x 61½". Quilted by Pam Clarke.*
Finished Block Size: 12"; Number of Blocks: 12

4. Join 4 of unit A, 4 of unit B, and a medium blue square to make a Star block.

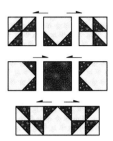
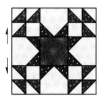

Make 12.

Assembly and Finishing

1. Join 3 sashing strips and 4 sashing squares to make 1 sashing row. Make 5 sashing rows.

Make 5.

2. Join 3 Star blocks and 4 sashing strips to make 1 row of blocks. Make 4 rows.

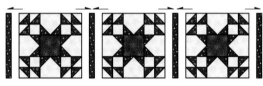

Make 4.

3. Join the 4 rows of blocks and 5 sashing rows.

Quilt Assembly Diagram

4. Referring to "Borders with Corner Squares" on page 56, measure and trim the border strips and sew them to the side edges of the quilt top first, and then to the top and bottom edges.

5. Piece and trim the backing fabric so it is approximately 6" larger than the quilt top.

6. Layer the quilt top with the batting and backing; baste. Quilt as desired.

7. Trim the batting and backing fabric so their edges are even with the quilt-top edges. Bind the quilt and add a label.

Spinning Stars

This quilt was designed for all of us who love hand appliqué and just can't find the time to do it. Machine blanket stitching is sewn around each of the connector designs and red stars. In addition to the simple but beautiful appliqué, this soothing quilt has a lot of visual movement and produces the illusion of antique pinwheels caught in a soft breeze. It would be equally stunning in a color palette that's just right for your home. My sister Diana Arkell will add this quilt to her new living room decor. —RW

Materials

All yardages are based on 42"-wide fabric.

- ✧ 2¾ yds. cream print for background and inner border #2
- ✧ 2¼ yds. green print for blocks, outer border, and connector design appliqués
- ✧ 1 yd. red for inner border #1, inner border #3, and star appliqués
- ✧ 4 yds. fabric for backing
- ✧ ⅝ yd. red print for binding
- ✧ 66" x 74" piece of batting
- ✧ 1¼ yds. fusible web for appliqué (optional)

Block Assembly

1. Using a ruler and a pencil, draw a diagonal line from corner to corner on the back of the background squares. Position a background square on top of a 2⅞" green square, right sides together. Stitch ¼" from each side of the marked line. Cut on the marked line. Press seams toward the green fabric and trim points. Make 120 half-square-triangle units.

Make 120.

2. Join 4 half-square-triangle units together as shown to make a center unit. Make 30 total.

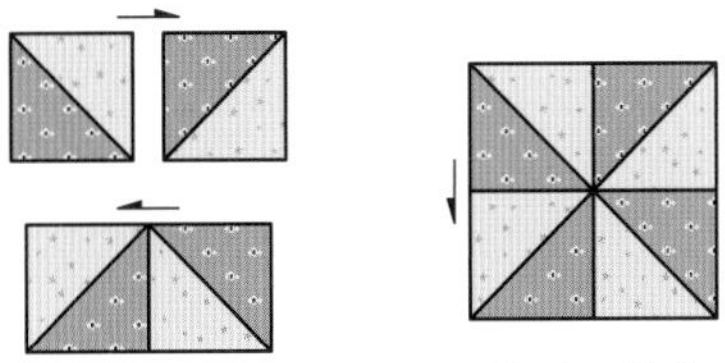

Center Unit
Make 30.

3. Using a ruler and a pencil, draw a diagonal line from corner to corner on the back of the 2½" green squares. Position a marked square on top of a 2½" x 6½" background rectangle, right sides together, aligning the right edges as shown. Stitch on the marked line. Trim seam ¼" from the stitching. Press seam toward the green fabric to make a side unit.

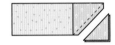

Side Unit
Make 120.

Cutting

Fabric	Used For	Number to Cut	Size to Cut	Second Cut
Cream print	Background	5 strips	2⅞" x 42"	60 squares, 2⅞" x 2⅞"
		8 strips	6½" x 42"	120 rectangles, 2½" x 6½"
	Inner border #2	6 strips	4" x 42"	
Green print	Blocks	5 strips	2⅞" x 42"	60 squares, 2⅞" x 2⅞"
		8 strips	2½" x 42"	120 squares, 2½" x 2½"
	Outer border	6 strips	4½" x 42"	
	Appliqué	20	Connector design template (page 25)	
Red	Inner border #1	6 strips	1½" x 42"	
	Inner border #3	6 strips	2" x 42"	
	Appliqué	18	Border star template (page 25)	
	Appliqué	20	Connector star template (page 25)	
Red print	Binding	7 strips	2½" x 42"	

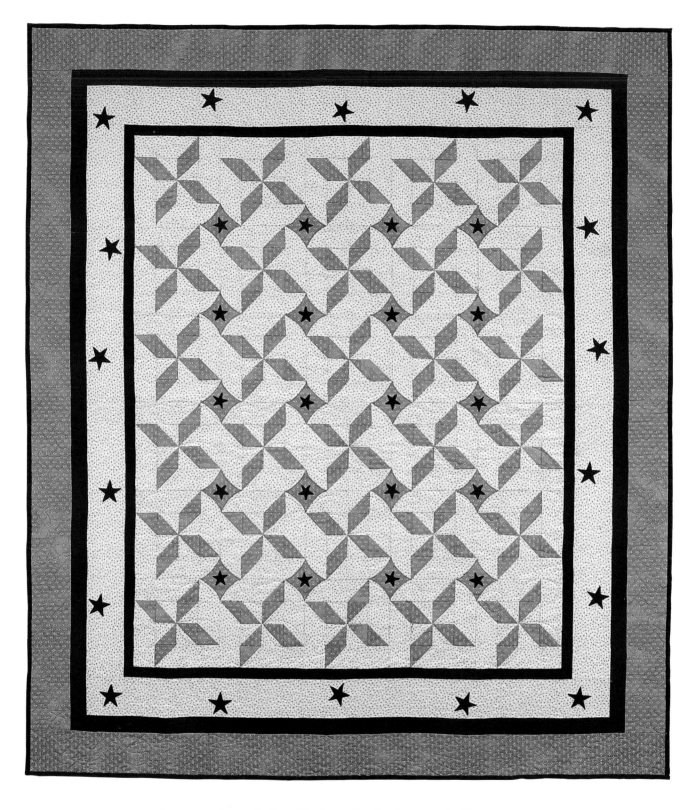

SPINNING STARS *by Retta Warehime, 60½" x 68½". Quilted by Pam Clarke.*

Finished Block Size: 8"; Number of Blocks: 30

4. Position a side unit on the right edge of a center unit, right sides together, aligning the green triangles at the lower edge. Stitch from midpoint of the center unit across the green triangles to the edge. Press seam away from center unit.

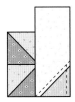 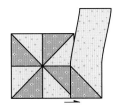

5. Join another side unit to the lower edge of the center unit, right sides together, aligning the green triangles at the lower left edge. Press seam away from the center unit. Repeat to join side units to the left and top edges of the center unit.

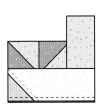 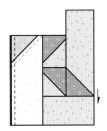

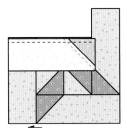 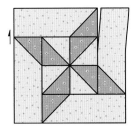

6. Complete the stitching, joining the right side unit to the center unit to make a Star block. Make 30 total.

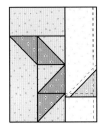 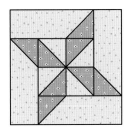

Make 30.

Assembly and Finishing

NOTE: *You can use your favorite appliqué method to add the connector designs and stars to your quilt. The quilt shown was made using fusible appliqué. (See "Appliqué Basics" on page 52 for details.) The appliqué shapes are secured in place permanently with machine blanket-stitch embroidery, but you may substitute the machine embroidery with hand blanket stitching if desired. See step 5 under "Fusible Appliqué" on page 55 for an illustration of the technique.*

1. Arrange the blocks into 6 rows of 5 blocks each. Sew the blocks together in horizontal rows. Press the seams in opposite directions from row to row.

2. Join the rows together in pairs, making 3 sections of 2 rows each.

   NOTE: *It is easiest to appliqué the connector designs and stars to 2 rows at a time.*

3. Select your favorite appliqué method. Then prepare 18 border stars, 20 connector stars, and 20 connector designs using the patterns on page 25. Pin or fuse the connector designs to the points where 4 blocks intersect; trim edges slightly to fit, if necessary. Hand or machine stitch in place. Appliqué the connector stars to the centers of the connector designs.

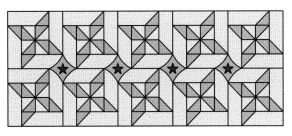

Make 3.

4. Join all 6 rows together and appliqué the remaining connector designs and connector stars in place.

5. Referring to "Butted-Corner Borders" on page 55, measure and trim the 1½" red inner border #1 strips and sew them to the side edges of the quilt top first, and then to the top and bottom

edges. Repeat for the 4" cream inner border #2, the 2" red inner border #3, and then the 4½" green outer border.

6. Using your favorite appliqué method, appliqué the border stars to the cream inner border #2. Place the stars randomly about 9" apart across the width of the border.

7. Piece and trim the backing fabric so it is approximately 6" larger than your quilt top.

8. Layer the quilt top with the batting and backing; baste. Quilt as desired.

9. Trim the batting and backing fabric so their edges are even with the quilt-top edges. Bind the edges and add a label.

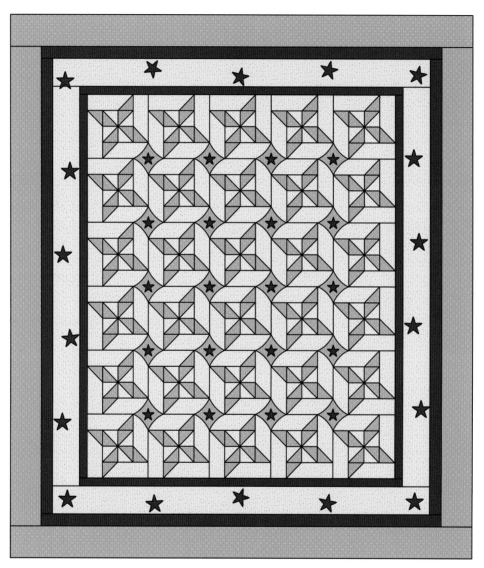

Quilt Assembly Diagram

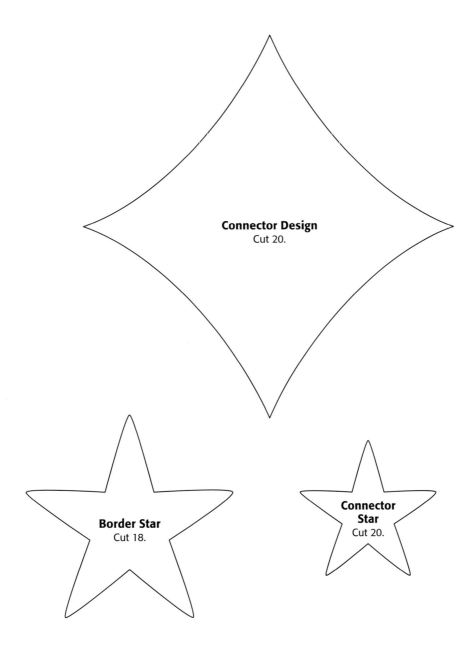

Connector Design
Cut 20.

Border Star
Cut 18.

Connector Star
Cut 20.

Button Basket

"Button Basket" embraces the very best days of summer. Its design is based on an antique quilt that featured straight-set repeats of the basket motif in true 1930s conversation prints and solids. Quick to piece, which is a must for busy quilters, and overflowing with soft, feminine colors, "Button Basket" even makes room for your favorite vintage button collection. If your household includes small children, please omit the buttons and replace them with contrasting fabric yo-yos. This is a good chance to take on an easy appliqué project that will achieve beautiful results. "Button Basket" will feel right at home in a special room at your house. —BK

Materials

All yardages are based on 42"-wide fabric, unless otherwise stated. Refer to the cutting list on page 29 for cutting instructions.

- ❖ 2⅞ yds. main floral fabric (F) for center square, borders, and binding
- ❖ ⅜ yd. each of 2 similar-value soft yellow floral fabrics (Y1 and Y2) for borders
- ❖ ⅝ yd. each of 2 similar-value soft pink floral fabrics (P1 and P2) for borders
- ❖ 1 fat quarter of very light pink or off-white for background of Basket block
- ❖ 1 fat quarter of deep yellow print for basket appliqué
- ❖ 1 fat quarter of medium green print (G) for cornerstones and leaf appliqués
- ❖ 12" square of deep pink with dots (PD) for cornerstones
- ❖ 12" square of deep pink stripe (PS) for cornerstones
- ❖ 12" square of dark pink for flower appliqués
- ❖ 4 yds. fabric for backing
- ❖ 70" x 70" piece of batting
- ❖ ½ yd. fusible web for appliqués
- ❖ 3 to 23 assorted vintage buttons for flower centers and cornerstones

Basket Block Assembly

NOTE: *You can use your favorite appliqué method to complete the Basket block. The quilt shown was made using freezer-paper appliqué. (See "Appliqué Basics" on page 52 for details.)*

1. Select your favorite appliqué method. Then prepare 1 basket, 2 leaf, and 3 flower appliqués, using the patterns on pages 31–32.

2. Fold the 15" background square in half on the diagonal and press. Unfold the square and turn it on point so the crease is vertical. Following the appliqué placement guide in step 3 at right, posi-

tion the basket, leaves, and then flowers on the background square. Use the crease as a guide for centering the appliqués.

3. Appliqué the pieces in place in the order indicated. Press lightly. Trim the square to 13½" x 13½".

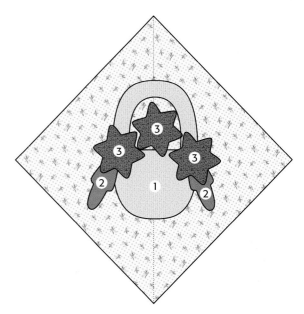

Appliqué Placement Guide

4. Join 2 main floral (F) triangles to opposite sides of the Basket block. Using a ruler and rotary cutter, trim the points. Join the remaining 2 floral triangles to the sides of the Basket block. Square up the block and carefully trim to measure 19½" x 19½".

NOTE: *The setting triangles are oversized to allow the Basket block to "float" in floral fabric.*

BUTTON BASKET *by Beth Merrill Kovich, 63½" x 63½". Machine quilted by Pam Clarke.*

Cutting

THE CENTER OF this quilt features an appliquéd Basket block, set on point and framed by triangles of the main floral fabric. After completion of the center square, five rounds of borders with cornerstones are added. The first and fifth borders each consist of 4 fabrics, and the second, third, and fourth borders use 3 fabrics. The quilt is finished with a wide outer border cut from the main floral fabric. To help keep the fabrics in order for the various border rounds, they have been labeled in the materials list on page 27 and the cutting list below. The same labels also appear in the quilt assembly diagram on page 30.

Fabric	Used For	Number to Cut	Size to Cut	Second Cut
Light pink or off-white	Background	1 square	15" x 15"	
Deep yellow print	Appliqué	1	Basket template (page 32)	
Dark pink	Appliqué	3	Flower template (page 31)	
Medium green print (G)	Cornerstones Appliqué	8 squares 2	3½" x 3½" Leaf template (page 31)	
Main floral (F)	Center square	2 squares	11" x 11"	◻
	Third border round	4 strips	3½" x 42"	4 strips, 3½" x 31½"
	Outer border	6 strips	7½" x 42"	2 strips, 7½" x 49½"* 2 strips, 7½" x 63½"*
	Binding	7 strips	2½" x 42"	
2 soft yellow florals (Y1 and Y2)	First border round	1 strip from each yellow	3½" x 42"	2 strips, 3½" x 19½", from each yellow
	Fourth border round	2 strips from each yellow	3½" x 42"	2 strips, 3½" x 37½", from each yellow
2 soft pink florals (P1 and P2)	Second border round	2 strips from each pink	3½" x 42"	2 strips, 3½" x 25½", from each pink
	Fifth border round	3 strips from each pink	3½" x 42"	2 strips, 3½" x 43½", from each pink*
Deep pink with dots (PD)	Cornerstones	6 squares	3½" x 3½"	
Deep pink with stripes (PS)	Cornerstones	6 squares	3½" x 3½"	

◻ Cut squares once diagonally.

***Note:** To cut these pieces longer than 42", join the strips on the diagonal as for binding strips; then cut to the appropriate length. See step 2 of "Mitered-Corner Binding" on page 58 for an illustration.

Quilt Assembly

1. Using the quilt assembly diagram as your guide, arrange the pieces for your quilt. Begin with the center square and build outward, paying attention to placement of the different cornerstones. A design wall is helpful for this step.

2. First border round: Join the 3½" x 19½" Y2 strips to the sides of the center square. Press seams toward the yellow fabric. Join the PD and PS cornerstones to the ends of the two 3½" x 19½" Y1 strips. Press seams toward the yellow fabric and add the strips to the top and bottom edges of the center square as shown in the assembly diagram. Press seams toward the yellow fabric.

3. Second border round: Join the 3½" x 25½" P2 strips to the sides of the quilt. Press seams toward the pink fabric. Join G cornerstones to the ends of the two 3½" x 25½" P1 strips. Press seams toward the pink fabric and add the strips to the top and bottom edges of the quilt as shown in the assembly diagram. Press seams toward the pink fabric.

Quilt Assembly Diagram

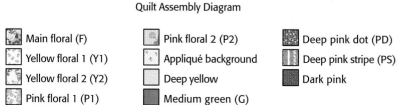

Main floral (F)

Yellow floral 1 (Y1)

Yellow floral 2 (Y2)

Pink floral 1 (P1)

Pink floral 2 (P2)

Appliqué background

Deep yellow

Medium green (G)

Deep pink dot (PD)

Deep pink stripe (PS)

Dark pink

4. Third border round: Join the 3½" x 31½" F strips to the sides of the quilt. Press seams toward the floral fabric. Join PD and PS cornerstones to the ends of the remaining two 3½" x 31½" F strips. Press seams toward the floral fabric and add the strips to the top and bottom edges of the quilt as shown in the assembly diagram. Press seams toward the floral fabric.

5. Fourth border round: Join the 3½" x 37½" Y1 strips to the sides of the quilt. Press seams toward the yellow fabric. Join G cornerstones to the ends of the two 3½" x 37½" Y2 strips. Press seams toward the yellow fabric and add strips to the top and bottom edges of the quilt as shown in the assembly diagram. Press seams toward the yellow fabric.

6. Fifth border round: Join the 3½" x 43½" P1 strips to the sides of the quilt. Press seams toward the pink fabric. Join PD and PS cornerstones to the ends of the two 3½" x 43½" P2 strips. Press seams toward the pink fabric and add the strips to the top and bottom edges of the quilt as shown in the assembly diagram. Press seams toward the pink fabric.

7. Join the 7½" x 49½" outer border strips to the sides of the quilt. Press seams toward the outer border. Join the 7½" x 63½" outer border strips to the top and bottom edges of the quilt. Press seams toward the outer border.

Finishing

1. Piece and trim the backing fabric so it is approximately 6" larger than your quilt top.

2. Layer the quilt top with the batting and backing; baste. Quilt as desired.

3. Trim the batting and backing so their edges are even with your quilt top. Sew buttons to the centers of the flowers and cornerstones, if desired. Bind the edges and add a label.

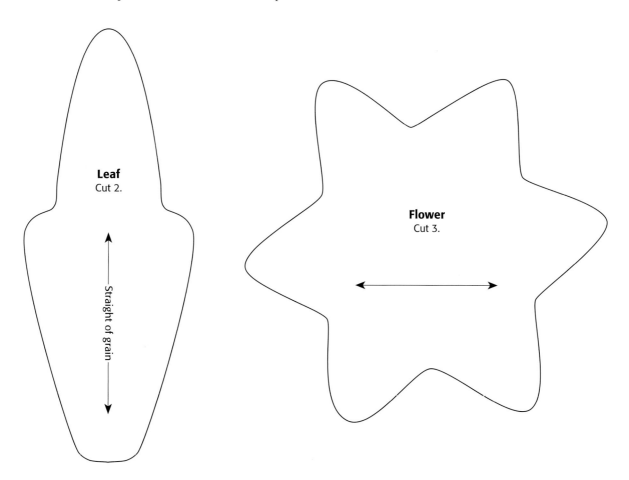

Leaf
Cut 2.

Straight of grain

Flower
Cut 3.

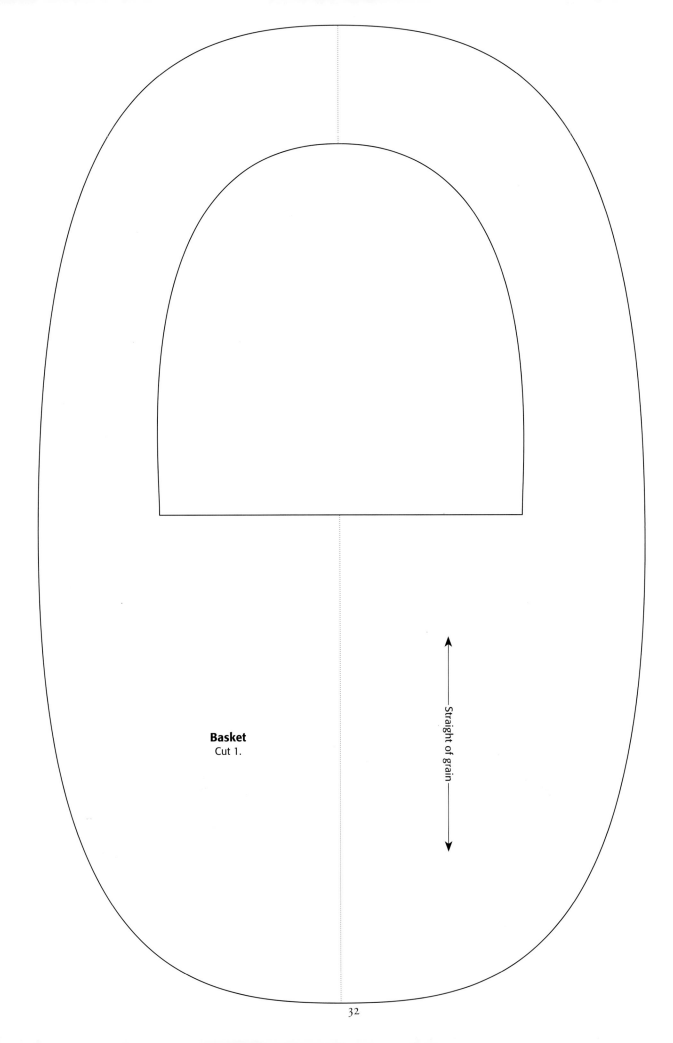

Basket
Cut 1.

Straight of grain

Plaid Goose

Plaids, plaids, plaids—can we ever have enough of them in our homes? This friendly quilt was designed using a single element from the classic block Goose Tracks. The layout is a little different than what you may be used to, but I think you'll agree that the finished product is worth the extra effort and sure to become a family favorite. By arranging the small blocks in a sixteen-unit grid (you'll make nine total), you will have an easier time matching seams and controlling the scrappiness of your finished quilt. The quilt shown contains nineteen different plaids in addition to the off-white plaid used for the background. To simplify things, I've written the instructions so that you will use fifteen of your favorite plaid fat quarters. —BK

Plaid Goose *by Beth Merrill Kovich, 60½" x 60½". Machine quilted by Pam Clarke.*
Finished Block Size: 5"; Number of Blocks: 144

Materials

All yardages are based on 42"-wide fabrics, unless otherwise stated. Choose a variety of dark, medium, and light fabrics.

- 2⅛ yds. off-white plaid for background and triangle units
- 15 fat quarters of assorted plaids for blocks and triangle units
- 4 yds. fabric for backing
- ⅝ yd. dark plaid for binding
- 66" x 66" piece of batting

Block Assembly

EACH OF the "hybrid" Goose Tracks blocks consists of a single plaid fabric and the background fabric and is easily made in pairs. Pay close attention to special pressing instructions as they have been written to minimize bulk and aid in the matching of points.

1. Using a ruler and a pencil, draw a diagonal line from corner to corner on the back of the 3¾" off-white squares. Position an off-white square on top of a plaid 3¾" square, right sides together. Stitch ¼" from each side of the marked line. Cut on the marked line; press seams open and trim points. Make 144 half-square-triangle units.

NOTE: *You will have 3 plaid squares left over.*

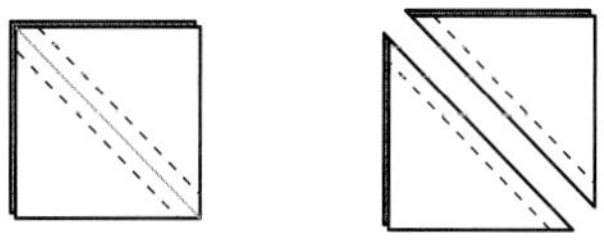

Make 144.

Cutting

Fabric	Used For	Number to Cut	Size to Cut	Second Cut
Off-white plaid	Background	12 strips	3" x 42"	144 squares, 3" x 3"
	Triangle units	8 strips	3¾" x 42"	72 squares, 3¾" x 3¾"
Each fat quarter	Triangle units	1 strip	3¾" x 20"	5 squares, 3¾" x 3¾"
	Blocks	2 strips	5⅞" x 20"	5 squares, 5⅞" x 5⅞" ◹
Dark plaid	Binding	7 strips	2½" x 42"*	

◹ Cut squares once diagonally.

* For straight-cut binding, cut strips 42" long across the width of the fabric. If you wish to use bias binding as I did for this quilt, cut 2½"-wide strips on the bias and join them end to end to make a continuous strip at least 250" long.

2. Cut the half-square-triangle units in half as shown to make 144 pairs of triangle units (288 total). Keep the pairs together.

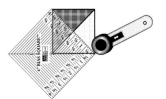

Make 144 pairs
(288 total).

3. Starting with a pair of triangle units from step 2, position the first triangle unit over a 3" background square, right sides together as shown. Note the location of the plaid half of the triangle unit. Align the corners at the lower right. Stitch along the right edge. Press seam toward the background fabric. Trim point.

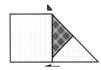

4. Position the remaining matching triangle unit over the same background square as shown. Note the location of the plaid half of the triangle unit. Stitch along the edge. Press seam toward the background fabric. Trim point to complete a pieced triangle unit. Make 144.

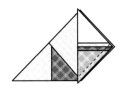
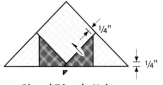
1/4"
1/4"
Pieced Triangle Unit
Make 144.

5. Sew a pieced triangle unit to a matching 5⅞" plaid triangle along the long edges. Press seam open and trim away points

NOTE: *You will have 6 plaid triangles left over.*

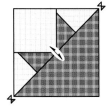
Make 144.

Assembly and Finishing

1. Arrange the blocks in 4 rows of 4 blocks each as shown. Sew the blocks together in horizontal rows, matching points (see tip on page 37 for further details). Press seams open. Join the rows together, matching points to make a 16-block unit. Press seams open. Make 9.

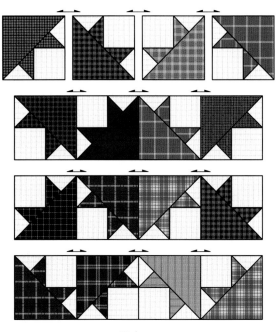
Make 9.

2. Arrange the 16-block units into 3 rows of 3 units each. Sew the units together in horizontal rows; press seam allowances open.

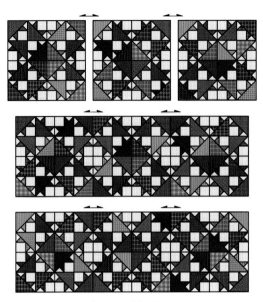

Quilt Assembly Diagram

3. Join the rows together; press seam allowances open.

4. Piece and trim the backing fabric so it is approximately 6" larger than your quilt top.

5. Layer the quilt top with the batting and backing; baste. Quilt as desired.

6. Trim the batting and backing fabric so their edges are even with your quilt top. Bind the edges and add a label.

TIP

To match 2 points perfectly along a seam, place blocks right sides together, and push a pin directly through the 2 points that need to match. Leave the pin upright in the blocks through the intersection as shown. Place pins on both sides of the matched point (as you normally would) to keep the seam from shifting. Sew the seam carefully, removing all the pins—including the positioning pin—as you come to them.

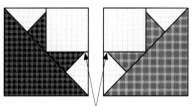

Points to be matched

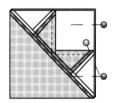

Positioning Pin through
Points on Both Blocks

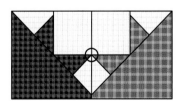

Accurate Match on Right Side of Fabric

Coffee and Cream

This quilt will be given to my "coffee and cream" friend Kathy Renzelman, with whom I always enjoy a trip to Starbucks. Each block is the result of an original positive/negative split Star block made from one light and one dark fabric. The quilt layout is a striking straight set that creates dramatic diagonal shadows when completed. Although this version has a scrappy country look, you could also achieve fantastic results with a collection of dark and light blues or even the increasingly popular batiks. —RW

Materials

All yardages are based on 42"-wide fabric unless otherwise stated.

- ✦ 10 assorted light-colored fat quarters for blocks
- ✦ 10 assorted dark-colored fat quarters for blocks
- ✦ 1 yd. gold print for outer border
- ✦ ½ yd. black-and-tan check for inner border
- ✦ 4 yds. fabric for backing
- ✦ ⅝ yd. dark print for binding
- ✦ 67" x 77" piece of batting

Block Assembly

NOTE: *For easiest assembly, the following step-by-step directions will guide you in making 3 blocks at a time with the same light-color and dark-color fabrics. You will make a total of 30 blocks—10 sets of 3 matching blocks.*

1. Using a ruler and a pencil, draw a diagonal line from corner to corner on the back of five 2⅞" light squares. Position each light square on top of a dark 2⅞" square, right sides together. Stitch ¼" from each side of the marked lines. Cut on the marked lines. Press seams toward the light fabric

and trim points to make 10 half-square-triangle units. You will use 9 and have 1 left over.

Make 9.

2. Using a ruler and a pencil, draw 2 diagonal lines from corner to corner on the back of two 3¼" light squares and two 3¼" dark squares. Pair each marked light square with an unmarked dark square and each marked dark square with an unmarked light square, right sides together, with the marked squares on top. Stitch ¼" from the marked lines as shown. Cut carefully on the marked lines to make 16 quarter-square triangles. You will only use 12 (6 of each kind) for each set of 3 blocks. Press seams toward the light fabric.

NOTE: *Sewing with both light and dark on top is what gives opposite dark and light positions.*

Make 6.

Make 6.

Cutting

NOTE: *For each fat quarter, cut the fabric pieces in the order listed.*

Fabric	Used For	Number to Cut	Size to Cut
Each fat quarter	Blocks	4 squares	3¼" x 3¼"
	Blocks	8 squares	2⅞" x 2⅞"
	Blocks	3 rectangles	2½" x 10½"
	Blocks	3 rectangles	2½" x 6½"
	Blocks	6 squares	2½" x 2½"
Black-and-tan check	Inner border	6 strips	2" x 42"
Gold print	Outer border	7 strips	4½" x 42"
Dark print	Binding	7 strips	2½" x 42"

COFFEE AND CREAM *by Retta Warehime, 61½" x 71½". Quilted by Pam Clarke.*
Finished Block Size: 10"; Number of Blocks: 30

3. Cut three 2⅞" light squares and three 2⅞" dark squares once diagonally. Join quarter-square triangles and light and dark triangles as shown to make the following units for star points.

Make 6.   Make 6.

4. Join 2 light star point units, 2 dark star point units, 3 half-square-triangle units, a 2½" light square, and a 2½" dark square to complete a star unit. Make 3 star units.

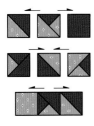

Star Unit
Make 3.

5. Using a ruler and a pencil, draw a diagonal line from corner to corner on the back of three 2½" dark squares and three 2½" light squares. Position a dark square on top of a 2½" x 10½" light rectangle, right sides together, aligning the right edges as shown. Stitch on the marked line. Trim seam ¼" from the stitching. Press seam toward the triangle. Make 3. Repeat to stitch the light squares on the 2½" x 10½" dark rectangles. Make 3.

NOTE: *Be careful to sew the squares to the rectangles as shown in the illustration. Sewing them on in another direction may result in the blocks not assembling properly.*

Make 3.

Make 3.

6. Join a 2½" x 6½" light rectangle to the left side of the star unit and a 2½" x 6½" dark rectangle to the right side of the unit. Join the rectangles from step 5 to the unit, sewing the rectangle with the dark triangle piece to the bottom and the rectangle with the light triangle piece to the top to make a Star block. Make 3 Star blocks.

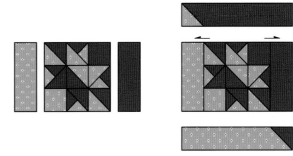

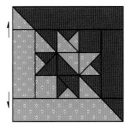

Star Block
Make 3.

7. Repeat steps 1–6 to make 10 sets of 3 matching Star blocks.

Assembly and Finishing

1. Arrange the blocks in 6 rows of 5 blocks each as shown. Sew the blocks into horizontal rows.

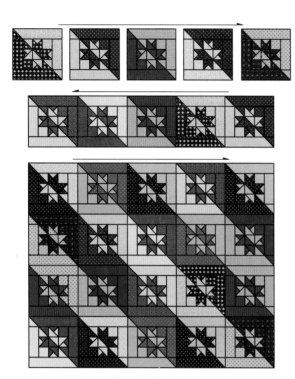

Quilt Assembly Diagram

2. Join the rows together.

3. Referring to "Butted-Corner Borders" on page 55, measure and trim the inner border strips and sew them to the side edges of the quilt top first, and then to the top and bottom edges. Repeat for the outer borders.

4. Piece and trim the backing fabric so it is approximately 6" larger than the quilt top.

5. Layer the quilt with the batting and backing; baste. Quilt as desired.

6. Trim the batting and backing fabric so their edges are even with the quilt-top edges.

7. Bind the quilt and add a label.

Tip

For a variation on this design, make this quilt with just two fabric colors. In the example shown, we substituted blue prints for the dark-colored fat quarters and solid cream for the light-colored fat quarters. We also used solid cream for the inner border and a blue print for the outer border and binding. Note that the blocks in this quilt are arranged with the blue prints on the lower right of each block. This creates diagonal shadows from the lower left to the upper right.

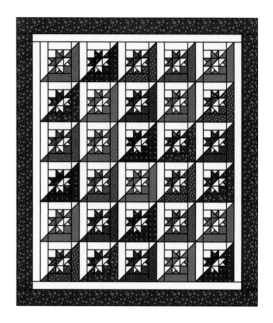

Beach Glass

Inspired by a block named Leavenworth Nine Patch, this soothing batik quilt is like a reflection of a rainy day at the beach—one of the best kinds of days to visit the beach in the Pacific Northwest, where I live. Big blocks are set on point and accented with subtle sashing. The quilt also features accent squares embedded in side setting triangles. Even though the overall effect is complicated in appearance, the only triangles you'll use for this quilt are along the outer edges. Choose a color palette that suits your favorite retreat spot, and soon you'll be able to curl up with your new quilt and a good book for an afternoon of reading. —BK

BEACH GLASS *by Beth Merrill Kovich, 56" x 56". Machine quilted by Frankie Schmitt.*

Finished Block and Accent-Square Sizes: Main Block: 10½" x 10½"; Accent Square: 4½" x 4½"

Number of Blocks and Accent Squares: Main Block: 13; Accent Square: 8

Materials

All yardages are based on 42"-wide fabrics, unless otherwise stated.

- ✧ 2⅞ yds. medium seaweed print batik for background, blocks, sashing squares, triangles, and binding
- ✧ 1⅛ yds. light mottled batik for blocks and sashing
- ✧ 1 fat quarter each of 6 solid jewel-tone batiks in medium purple, dark purple, turquoise, green, blue-green, and fuchsia for blocks and sashing squares
- ✧ 3¾ yds. fabric for backing
- ✧ 62" x 62" piece of batting

Block Assembly

YOU WILL be making the Leavenworth Nine Patch blocks in stages. The accent squares are used later in the side setting triangles but are made at the same time as the blocks. You will need to make the following number of blocks and accent squares from each fat quarter color as indicated below:

Medium purple (2 blocks, 2 accent squares)
Dark purple (2 blocks, 2 accent squares)
Turquoise (2 blocks, 2 accent squares)
Green (2 blocks, 2 accent squares)
Blue-green (2 blocks)
Fuchsia (3 blocks)

Cutting

Fabric	Used For	Number to Cut	Size to Cut	Second Cut
Light mottled batik	Blocks	5 strips	2" x 42"	94 squares, 2" x 2"
	Sashing	12 strips	2" x 42"	36 rectangles, 2" x 11"
Each purple fat quarter	Blocks and sashing squares	6 strips	2" x 20"	22 squares, 2" x 2" 16 rectangles, 2" x 3½"
Turquoise fat quarter	Blocks	6 strips	2" x 20"	18 squares, 2" x 2" 16 rectangles, 2" x 3½"
Green fat quarter	Blocks	6 strips	2" x 20"	18 squares, 2" x 2" 16 rectangles, 2" x 3½"
Blue-green fat quarter	Blocks	4 strips	2" x 20"	14 squares, 2" x 2" 12 rectangles, 2" x 3½"
Fuchsia fat quarter	Blocks and sashing squares	6 strips	2" x 20"	25 squares, 2" x 2" 18 rectangles, 2" x 3½"
Medium seaweed print	Blocks and sashing squares	16 strips	2" x 42"	78 rectangles, 2" x 5" 26 rectangles, 2" x 3½" 46 squares, 2" x 2"
	Side setting triangles	4 squares	14" x 14"	⊠
	Corner triangles	2 squares	13½" x 13½"	◺
	Binding	6 strips	2½" x 42"	

◺ Cut squares once diagonally.

⊠ Cut squares twice diagonally.

1. Join 2" light mottled batik squares to 2" fat quarter squares. Press seams away from the light batik to make 94 total of unit A.

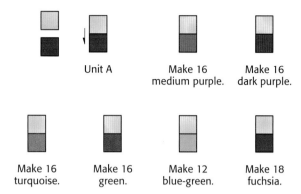

Unit A

Make 16 medium purple.

Make 16 dark purple.

Make 16 turquoise.

Make 16 green.

Make 12 blue-green.

Make 18 fuchsia.

2. Join matching pairs of unit A, turning 1 to make a four-patch unit (unit B) as shown. Make 34 total of unit B. Press seam to one side. You will have 26 of unit A left over; these will be used in step 4.

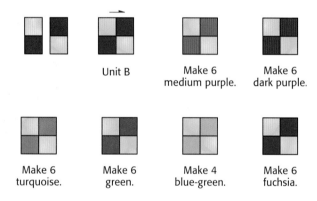

Unit B

Make 6 medium purple.

Make 6 dark purple.

Make 6 turquoise.

Make 6 green.

Make 4 blue-green.

Make 6 fuchsia.

3. Join two 2" x 3½" rectangles of matching fat quarter fabric and one 2" square of seaweed print to unit B to make unit C. Make 34 total of unit C. The C units are used as accent squares and are also used to construct the blocks. Set aside the

required number of accent squares (quantities listed by color on page 45).

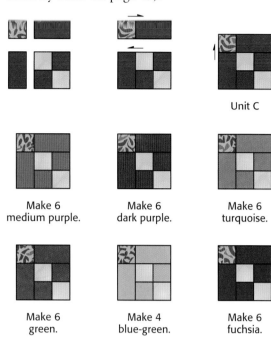

Unit C

Make 6 medium purple.

Make 6 dark purple.

Make 6 turquoise.

Make 6 green.

Make 4 blue-green.

Make 6 fuchsia.

4. Join a 2" x 3½" rectangle of matching fat quarter fabric, a 2" x 3½" seaweed print rectangle, and a 2" x 5" seaweed print rectangle to the remaining unit A pieces as shown to make unit D. Make 26 total of unit D.

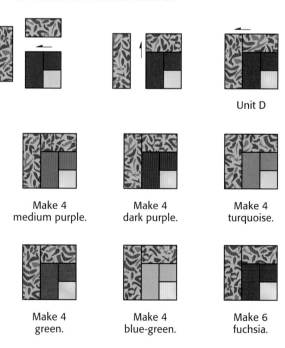

Unit D

Make 4 medium purple.

Make 4 dark purple.

Make 4 turquoise.

Make 4 green.

Make 4 blue-green.

Make 6 fuchsia.

5. Arrange matching pairs of unit C and unit D, one 2" square from the same fat quarter used in units C and D, and four 2" x 5" rectangles of

seaweed print to form a Leavenworth Nine Patch block. Sew the units together into rows, and then sew the rows together. Repeat to make 13 blocks. Refer to the quantities listed by color on page 45 if you need help.

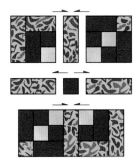 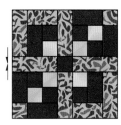

Make 13.

Assembly and Finishing

A DESIGN wall or a large, flat space is essential for the layout of this quilt because the blocks are set on point with sashing, and diagonal rows are used for assembly. Refer to the quilt assembly diagram for suggested color placement and layout of the blocks, light batik sashing strips, seaweed print and colored sashing squares, accent square triangles, and corner triangles. Follow the diagram carefully as no 2 diagonal rows are identical. Be-fore the quilt is assembled, you will make the special side setting triangles that contain the accent squares.

1. Make the special side setting triangles using the 8 reserved accent squares and the 16 side setting triangles. These triangles are intentionally cut large to complete the border while framing the accent square. Align 1 short side of the side set-ting triangle with a side of the accent square that does not contain the seaweed print square. Sew, press, and trim the triangle as shown. Join the second triangle to the pieced unit as shown. Make 8 accent square triangles.

 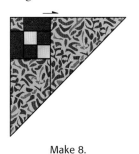

Trim.   Make 8.

2. Arrange the blocks on point. Position the sashing strips and sashing squares around the blocks. Sew the sashing strips between the blocks and at the end of each row. Sew the sashing strips and sashing squares together to make sashing rows. Press seams toward sashing.

3. Sew the sashing rows and rows of blocks to-gether, matching seam intersections. Add the special side setting triangles to the ends of the rows. Press seams toward the sashing.

4. Join the rows, adding the corner triangles last.

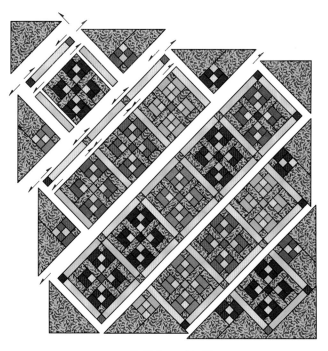

Quilt Assembly Diagram

NOTE: *The corner triangles are intentionally over-sized and will be trimmed after quilting. Press seam allowances in one direction.*

5. Piece and trim the backing fabric so it is approx-imately 6" larger than your quilt top.

6. Layer the quilt top with the batting and backing; baste. Quilt as desired.

7. Trim the quilt to measure 56" x 56"; square up the corners of the quilt as necessary. Bind the edges and add a label.

Quiltmaking Essentials

Don't skip this section! On the pages that follow, you'll find valuable information for the successful completion of your snuggle-up quilt. Designed for both beginners and experienced quiltmakers, this section is a perfect reference tool for everyone. From gathering your tools to finishing your quilt, these handy tips will help you brush up on the basics.

Fabrics

We always use 100 percent–cotton fabrics. We trust that they will last and know that they are easy to work with. Although most of the quilts in this book were made from regular cotton fabric, all of the designs can also be made in cotton flannel for an extra-cozy quilt.

Sufficient yardage requirements are provided for all the projects in this book and are based on 42"-wide fabrics that provide at least 40" of usable fabric after prewashing and after selvages have been trimmed away. To vary the look of any design, use an assortment of scraps and purchase only those fabrics you need to complete the project you are making. By adding fabrics from your stash, you will be enhancing the personal feel of your quilt. Challenge yourself to make a scrappy quilt.

We suggest prewashing all fabrics to test for colorfastness. This step also removes any excess dyes that may be in the fabric. Always iron your fabrics before cutting to ensure accuracy. Some lighter-weight fabrics benefit from being pressed with a light spray starch as well. Alternately, a crinkled, instant-vintage look is guaranteed if you choose to wash your fabrics only after the quilt is completed. We like both looks and encourage you to experiment.

Supplies

Sewing machine: To machine piece, you'll need a sewing machine that has a good straight stitch. You'll also need a walking foot or darning foot if you plan to machine quilt.

Rotary-cutting tools: You'll need a rotary cutter, cutting mat, and clear acrylic ruler. Rotary-cutting rulers are available in a variety of sizes, including 6" x 24", 12" x 12", and 15" x 15". Our current favorites also include 4" x 14" and 6" x 12".

Thread: Use a good-quality, all-purpose cotton thread. We find that we use off-white, light gray, and black thread most often.

Needles: Always use a fresh needle for each new project. For machine piecing, a size 10/70 or 12/80 works well. For machine quilting, a larger needle, such as a 14/90, works best. For hand appliqué, choose a needle that will glide easily through the edges of the appliqué pieces. Size 10 (fine) to size 12 (very fine) needles are good choices.

Pins: Long, fine silk pins slip easily through fabric, making them perfect for patchwork. Smaller, ½"- to ¾"-long sequin pins work best for appliqué.

Scissors: Use your best scissors only for cutting fabric. Use craft scissors to cut paper, fusible web, and template plastic.

Template plastic: Clear or frosted plastic, available at quilt shops, makes durable, accurate templates.

Seam ripper: We use one every time we sew. The sharper, the better, in order to get back to your sewing more quickly.

Marking tools: A variety of tools are available to mark fabric when tracing around templates or marking quilting designs. We caution you to test your quilt marking tool on a scrap of fabric to make sure you can remove the marks easily.

Rotary Cutting

WE LOVE the speed and accuracy of rotary cutting and rely on it whenever possible. All measurements include standard ¼"-wide seam allowances. If you are unfamiliar with rotary cutting, read the brief introduction that follows. For more detailed information, see *Shortcuts: A Concise Guide to Rotary Cutting* by Donna Lynn Thomas (Martingale & Company, 1999).

1. Fold the fabric in half, matching selvages. Align the crosswise and lengthwise grains as well as possible. Place the fabric, folded edge nearest you, on the cutting mat. Align a square ruler along the folded edge of the fabric. Place a long, straight ruler to the left of the square ruler, just covering the uneven raw edges of the left side of the fabric.

    Move the square ruler aside and cut along the right edge of the long ruler, rolling the rotary cutter away from you. Discard this strip. (Reverse this procedure if you are left-handed.)

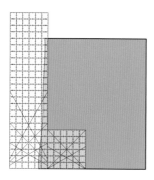

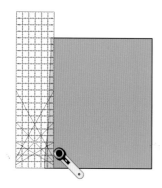

2. To cut strips across the fabric, align the newly cut edge of the fabric with the ruler markings at the required width. For example, to cut a 3"-wide strip, place the 3" ruler mark on the edge of the fabric.

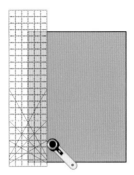

3. To cut squares, cut strips in the required widths, and trim the selvage ends of the strips. Align the left edge of the strips with the correct ruler markings. The sides of the square should have the same measurement as the width of the strips. Crosscut the strips into squares, cutting squares until you have the number needed.

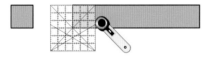

4. To cut a half-square triangle, begin by cutting a square ⅞" larger than the desired finished size of the short side of the triangle. Then cut the square once diagonally, from corner to corner. Each square yields 2 half-square triangles. The short sides of each triangle are on the straight grain of the fabric.

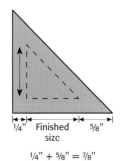

¼" Finished size ⅝"

¼" + ⅝" = ⅞"

5. To cut a quarter-square triangle, begin by cutting a square 1¼" larger than the desired finished size of the long edge of the triangle. Then cut the square twice diagonally, from corner to corner. Each square yields 4 quarter-square triangles. The long side of each triangle is on the straight grain of the fabric.

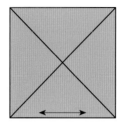

⅝" Finished size ⅝"

Machine Piecing

ALL OF the quilts in this book are designed for the quickest piecing possible. We always take the time to establish an exact ¼"-wide seam on our machines and we encourage you to do the same. Your machine may have a special patchwork or quilting foot that measures exactly ¼" from the center needle position to the edge of the foot. This feature allows you to use the edge of the presser foot to guide the fabric for a perfect ¼"-wide seam allowance.

If your machine doesn't have such a foot, create a seam guide by placing the edge of a piece of tape, moleskin, or a magnetic seam guide ¼" away from the needle.

By determining an exact ¼"-wide seam for your piecing, you will have better luck in constructing your quilt accurately.

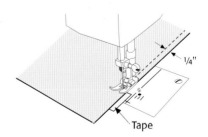

¼"

Tape

Chain Piecing

CHAIN PIECING speeds assembly and conserves thread. It's especially useful when you're making many identical units, such as the four-patch units in "Opening Day" on page 8.

1. Stitch a pair of pieces together, sewing from cut edge to cut edge, using 12 to 15 stitches per inch. Stop sewing at the end of the seam, but do not cut the thread.

2. Place the next pair of pieces under the presser foot, as close as possible to the first pair, and sew a seam. Continue feeding pairs through the machine without cutting the threads in between the pairs.

3. When all pairs are sewn together, remove the chain from the machine and clip the threads between the pairs of sewn pieces.

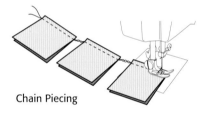

Chain Piecing

Pressing

THE TRADITIONAL rule in quiltmaking is to press seams to one side, toward the darker color wherever possible. First press the seams flat from the wrong side of the fabric; then press the seams in the desired direction from the right side. Press carefully to avoid distorting the shapes. There is always an exception to the rule. For example, "Plaid Goose" on page 33 has specific pressing instructions to aid in the matching of seams.

When joining two seamed units, plan ahead and press the seam allowances in opposite directions, as shown. This reduces bulk and makes it easier to match the seams. The seam allowances will butt against each other where two seams meet, making it easier to sew units with perfectly matched seam intersections.

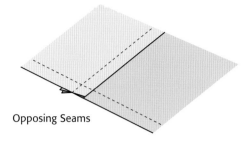

Opposing Seams

Appliqué Basics

WE'VE PROVIDED general instructions here for freezer-paper and fusible appliqué. Always use your favorite method regardless of what method is described in the project. Just be sure to adapt the pattern pieces and project instructions as necessary.

MAKING TEMPLATES

You'll need to make templates of the appliqué patterns. We prefer to make our templates from clear plastic because plastic templates are more durable and accurate than those made from other materials. And, since you can see through the plastic, it is easy to trace the templates accurately from the book page.

Place template plastic over each pattern piece and trace with a fine-line permanent marker. Do not add seam allowances. Cut out the templates on the drawn lines. You need only one template for each different motif or shape. Write the pattern name and grain-line arrow (if applicable) on the template.

FREEZER-PAPER APPLIQUÉ

Freezer paper, which is coated on one side, is often used to help make perfectly shaped appliqués. With this method, the seam allowances are turned under before the appliqué is stitched to the background fabric.

1. Place the plastic template on the dull side of the freezer paper and trace around the template with a sharp pencil. Or place the freezer paper, shiny side down, on top of the pattern and trace.

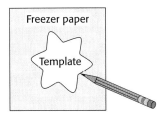

2. Cut around the traced design on the marked pencil line. Do not add seam allowances.

3. Position the shiny side of the paper on the wrong side of your appliqué fabric, and iron the freezer-paper design in place with a hot, dry iron.

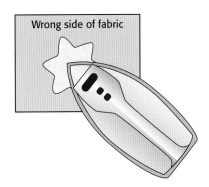

4. Cut around the freezer-paper shape, adding ¼" seam allowances around all edges.

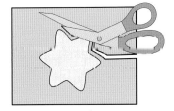

5. Fold the seam allowances over the freezer-paper edges and baste by hand or use a fabric glue stick to secure them in place. Clip inside points and fold in excess fabric at outside points.

6. Pin or baste the appliqué design to the background fabric or block. Secure the design in place, using the traditional appliqué stitch (see below).

7. Remove any basting stitches. Cut a slit in the background fabric behind the appliqué and remove the freezer paper with tweezers. If you used a fabric glue stick, soak the piece in warm water for a few minutes, and then remove the freezer paper.

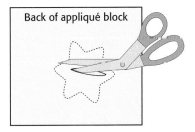

TRADITIONAL APPLIQUÉ STITCH

Use the traditional appliqué stitch or blind stitch to hand-sew all appliqué shapes in place, including pieces with sharp points and curves.

1. Thread a needle with a single strand of thread, about 18" long, in a color that closely matches the color of your appliqué. Knot the end.

2. Conceal the knot by slipping the needle into the seam allowance from the wrong side of the appliqué piece and bringing it out on the fold line.

3. Stitch from right to left if you are right-handed, or from left to right if you are left-handed. Insert the needle into the background right next to where the needle came out of the appliqué fabric and bring the needle up through the edge of the appliqué, about ⅛" away to complete the first stitch. As you bring the needle up, pierce the basted edge of the appliqué piece, catching only 1 or 2 threads.

4. Take a second stitch into the background block right next to where the thread came up through the appliqué. Bring the needle up about ⅛" away from the previous stitch, again catching the edge of the appliqué.

5. Pull the thread snug and continue stitching.

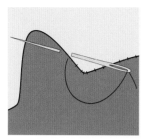

NOTE: *The stitches in these appliqué illustrations are drawn large to indicate placement. The stitches should not show in the completed work.*

6. To end your stitching, pull the needle through to the wrong side. Behind the appliqué piece, take 2 small stitches, making knots by taking your needle through the loops.

FUSIBLE APPLIQUÉ

Fusible web is used to adhere appliqués to a background quickly and easily. Stitching around the appliqué shapes is suggested. Use the patterns exactly as they appear, as the projects in this book do not use patterns that are directional (no need to reverse templates).

Refer to the manufacturer's directions when applying fusible web to your fabrics; each brand is a little different and pressing it too long may result in fusible web that doesn't stick well.

1. Trace the appliqué design on the paper backing side of the fusible web. Cut around the shape, leaving at least ¼" around all edges.

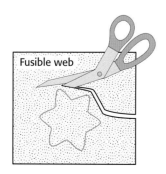

2. Fuse the appliqué shape to the wrong side of your chosen fabric.

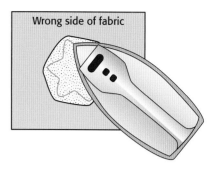

3. Cut out the appliqué shape exactly on the marked line.

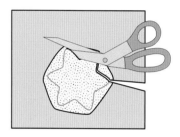

4. Remove the paper backing from the appliqué, position the shape on the background fabric, and fuse it in place with your iron.

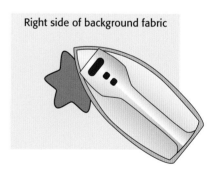

5. Add decorative stitches by hand or machine around the edges of the fused appliqués, if desired. Commonly used stitches include the satin stitch and the blanket stitch. The appliqués in "Spinning Stars" (page 20) are edged with machine blanket stitching. You may also blanket stitch by hand as shown below.

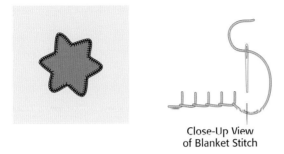

Close-Up View
of Blanket Stitch

Adding Borders

ALWAYS MEASURE your quilt before cutting or adding border strips. We find that the edges of a quilt often measure slightly longer than the distance through the quilt center, due to natural stretching during construction. We measure the quilt top through the center in both directions to determine how long to cut the border strips. This step ensures that your finished quilt will be as straight and as "square" as possible.

All the quilts in this book call for plain border strips. The strips are cut along the crosswise grain and seamed where extra length is needed.

Borders in this book may have butted corners or corner squares. Refer to the quilt pattern you are following to see which corner treatment you need.

BUTTED-CORNER BORDERS

1. Measure the length of the quilt top through the center, and cut 2 border strips to that measurement, piecing as necessary. Mark the midpoints of the border strips and quilt top by folding each in half and creasing or pinning the centers. Then pin the border strips to opposite sides of the quilt top, matching the center marks and ends and easing as necessary. Sew the side border strips in place. Press the seams toward the border strips.

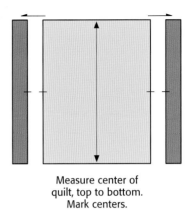

Measure center of
quilt, top to bottom.
Mark centers.

2. Measure the width of the quilt top through the center, including the side borders just added. Cut 2 border strips to that measurement, piecing as necessary. Mark the midpoints of the quilt along the top and bottom edges and the midpoints of the border strips. Pin the borders to the top and bottom edges of the quilt top, matching the center marks and ends and easing as necessary. Sew the border strips in place. Press the seams toward the border strips.

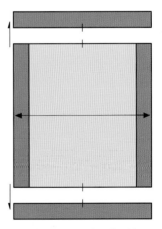

Measure center of quilt, side to
side, including border strips.
Mark centers.

BORDERS WITH CORNER SQUARES

1. Measure the width and length of the quilt top through the center.

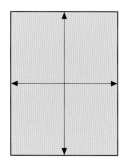

Measure center of quilt top
in both directions.

2. Cut border strips to those measurements, piecing as necessary. Mark the midpoints of the border strips and quilt top by folding each in half and creasing or pinning the centers. Pin the side borders to opposite sides of the quilt top, matching center marks and ends and easing as necessary. Sew the side border strips in place. Press the seams toward the border strips.

3. Cut corner squares of the required size, which is the cut width of the border strips. Sew a corner square to each end of the remaining 2 border strips. Press the seam allowances toward the border strips. Pin the border strips to the top and bottom edges of the quilt top. Match midpoints, seams between the border strips and corner squares, and ends, easing as necessary. Sew the border strips in place. Press the seams toward the border strips.

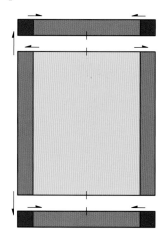

Preparing to Quilt

FOLLOW THE directions in this section for marking, layering, basting, and quilting if you plan to quilt by hand or on your home sewing machine. If you plan to have a professional machine quilter quilt your project, check with that person before preparing your finished quilt top in any way. All the quilts in this book were quilted by professional long-arm machine quilters. To find a long-arm quilter in your area, check with your local quilt shop for referrals or consult "Resources" on page 61. In our experience, quilts do not need to be layered, basted, or marked for long-arm machine quilting.

MARKING THE QUILTING LINES

Depending on the type of quilting you will be doing, you may need to mark quilting designs on the quilt top before you baste the quilt layers together. Marking is not necessary if you plan to quilt in the ditch (along the seam lines) or outline quilt a uniform distance from the seam lines. For more complex quilting designs, however, mark the quilt top before the quilt is layered with batting and backing.

Select a marking tool that will be visible on your fabric and test it on fabric scraps to be sure the marks can be removed easily. Masking tape can be used to mark straight quilting lines. Tape only small sections at a time and remove the tape when you stop at the end of a quilting session, or the sticky residue may be difficult to remove from the fabric.

Layering and Basting the Quilt

After you complete the quilt top and mark it for quilting, assemble your very own quilt "sandwich," which consists of the backing, batting, and the quilt top. The quilt backing and batting should be cut about 6" larger than the quilt top. For large quilts, it is usually necessary to sew 2 or 3 lengths of fabric together to make a backing that is large enough. Always trim away the selvages before piecing the lengths together. Press the seams open to make quilting easier by minimizing bulk.

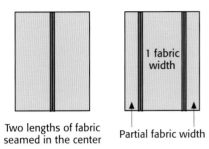

Two lengths of fabric seamed in the center   Partial fabric width

Batting comes packaged in standard bed sizes, or it can be purchased by the yard in many different weights or thicknesses. A thinner batting is better, however, if you intend to quilt by hand or machine and it also has nicer drape.

1. Lay the backing wrong side up on a flat, clean surface. Secure in place with pins or masking tape, taking care not to stretch the backing out of shape.

2. Spread the batting over the backing fabric, smoothing out any wrinkles.

3. Center the pressed quilt top over the batting. Smooth out any wrinkles and make sure the quilt-top edges are parallel to the edges of the backing.

4. Baste the layers together with a needle and thread, starting in the center and working diagonally to each corner. Then baste a grid of horizontal and vertical lines 6" to 8" apart. Finish by basting around the edges.

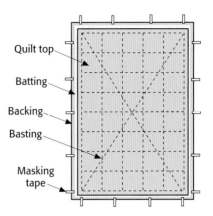

NOTE: *For machine quilting, you may baste the layers with #2 rustproof safety pins. Place the pins about 6" to 8" apart, away from your intended quilting lines.*

Machine Quilting

MACHINE QUILTING is suitable for all types of quilts, especially snuggle-up quilts. With machine quilting, you can quickly complete quilts in a way that will withstand repeated washings and all the love your family dishes out.

Marking the quilting design is optional. You will only need to mark your quilt if you select a complex design or plan to follow a grid. In most cases, the quilts in this book lend themselves to stitching in the ditch, outline quilting, or free-motion quilting in a random pattern.

For straight-line quilting (such as in the ditch), it is extremely helpful to have a walking foot to help feed the quilt layers through the machine without shifting or puckering. Some machines have a built-in walking foot; other machines require a separate attachment.

For free-motion quilting, you will need to use a darning foot and drop or cover the feed dogs on your machine. Consult your sewing machine instruction manual if you need help. With free-motion quilting, you guide the fabric, following the direction of the design, rather than turn the fabric under the needle. Use free-motion quilting to outline quilt a fabric motif or to create stippling or other curved designs.

If, like us, you prefer to have your quilt quilted by a professional so you can move along to your next project, establish a relationship with a local long-arm professional. Ask your friends, your teachers, and your local quilt shop for referrals. A local quilting guild may also be able to offer assistance.

Finishing Techniques

YOU'RE IN the final stretch now! Follow these simple steps for adding a hanging sleeve (optional), binding and a label. Get set to enjoy your snuggle-up quilt.

BINDING

Our preferred type of binding is called French double-fold binding. Instructions are given for both a mitered-corner and a lapped-corner French double-fold binding. Both corner treatments have been used for the quilts in this book. All bindings in this book were cut 2½" wide across the width of fabric and then pieced, with the exception of the binding on "Plaid Goose" (page 33). The binding for this quilt was cut on the bias. You will need enough strips to go around the perimeter of the quilt, plus 10" for seams and finishing the corners.

Mitered-Corner Binding

1. Trim the batting and backing even with the edges of the quilt top. If you plan to add a hanging sleeve, do so now before attaching the binding (see "Adding a Hanging Sleeve," page 59).

2. Join the binding strips together to make one continuous strip. Sew the strips together at right angles, right sides together, by stitching across the corner as shown. Trim ¼" from the stitching. Press the seams open.

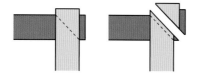

3. Fold the binding strip in half lengthwise, wrong sides together, and press. Turn under ¼" at a 45° angle at one end of the strip, and press. Turning the end under at an angle distributes the bulk so you will have a smoother connection where the 2 ends of the binding meet.

4. Starting away from a corner on one side of the quilt and using a ¼"-wide seam allowance, stitch the binding to the quilt, keeping the raw edges even with the quilt top edge. End the stitching ¼" from the corner of the quilt and backstitch. Clip the thread.

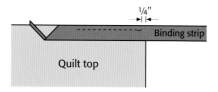

5. Turn the quilt 90° so that you'll be stitching down the next side. Fold the binding up, away from the quilt. Fold the binding back down onto itself, aligning the raw edges with the quilt top edge, adjacent the side you just stitched. Begin stitching ¼" from the corner, backstitching to secure the stitches. Repeat the process on the remaining edges and corners of the quilt.

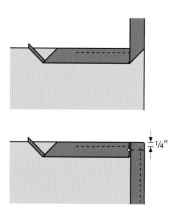

6. When you reach the starting point of the binding, stop stitching. Overlap the starting edge of the binding by about 1" and cut away any excess binding, trimming the end at a 45° angle. Tuck the end of the binding into the fold and finish sewing the binding in place.

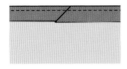

7. Fold the binding over the raw edges of the quilt to the back of the quilt, so the folded edge just covers the row of machine stitching. Blindstitch the binding in place. A miter will form at each corner. Blindstitch the mitered corners in place.

Lapped-Corner Binding

1. Follow steps 1 and 2 on page 58 for mitered-corner binding. Fold the binding strip in half lengthwise, wrong sides together, and press. Measure the quilt top vertically through the center and cut 2 strips of binding to this length for the side bindings. Use a ¼" seam allowance to stitch the binding to the sides of the quilt, keeping the raw edges of the binding even with the trimmed edges of the quilt. Fold the binding over the edges of the quilt to the back of the quilt, with the folded edge covering the row of machine stitching. Blindstitch both sections of binding in place.

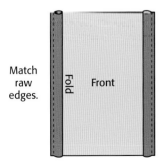

Match raw edges.

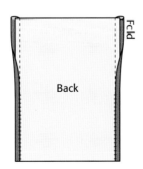

2. Measure the quilt top horizontally through the center and cut 2 strips from the binding to this measurement, plus 1". Unfold binding at ends; then fold in and press ½" on each end. Refold binding lengthwise and press ends. Stitch the binding to the top and bottom edges of the quilt, keeping raw edges even with quilt-top edges. Fold the binding to the back side and finish as for the side bindings. Slipstitch the ends closed.

Back

ADDING A HANGING SLEEVE

If your snuggle-up quilt will live on your wall instead of the sofa for most of its life, we suggest adding a permanent hanging sleeve to your quilt. A hanging sleeve creates a safe way to hold the rod you'll use to display your quilt on the wall. The addition of a hanging sleeve makes it simple to change the look of a room by rotating your quilt collection on a single rod.

1. From the leftover quilt backing fabric, cut a strip 6" to 8" wide and 1" shorter than the width of your quilt. Fold the ends under ½", then ½" again to make a hem. Stitch in place.

Fold ends under ½" twice.

2. Fold the fabric strip in half lengthwise, wrong sides together, and baste the raw edges to the top of the quilt back. The top edge of the sleeve will be secured when the binding is sewn on the quilt.

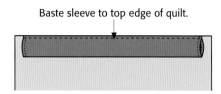

Baste sleeve to top edge of quilt.

3. After the binding has been attached, finish the sleeve by blindstitching the bottom in place. But, before sewing the bottom edge in place, push the sleeve up just a bit to provide a little give; this will keep the hanging rod from putting strain on the quilt.

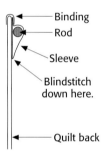

Binding
Rod
Sleeve
Blindstitch down here.
Quilt back

SIGNING YOUR QUILT

Please be sure to sign and date your new snuggle-up quilt. You've worked hard on it and you deserve the recognition. Besides, if the quilt is a gift, your family and friends will treasure the extra bit of effort you put into personalizing your creation just for them. The essential information to include is the name of the quilt, your name, the quilter's name (if different from you), your city and state, the date, and the intended recipient. Don't let your quilt be a mystery for future generations to puzzle over! Use a fine-tipped, permanent fabric marker to record all of the pertinent information on a piece of fabric. You can stabilize the label fabric for easier writing by ironing a piece of freezer paper to the back side. Once you've recorded your information, remove the freezer paper, and attach the label to the back of the quilt. You may also type or embroider your information on fabric before attaching to the back of your finished quilt, but we find the marker method most efficient.

Crossing Paths
by
Retta Warehime,
Kennewick, WA, 2002,
$57^{1}/_{2}$" x $81^{1}/_{2}$".
Quilted by Pam Clarke.

Bibliography

Havig, Bettina. *Carrie Hall Blocks.* Paducah, Ky.: American Quilter's
Society, 1999.

Hopkins, Judy. *Around the Block with Judy Hopkins.* Woodinville, Wash.:
Martingale & Company, 1994.

Thomas, Donna Lynn. *Shortcuts: A Concise Guide to Rotary Cutting.*
Woodinville, Wash.: Martingale & Company, 1999.

Resources

THE FOLLOWING BUSINESSES provide machine quilting services:

Pam Clarke
Designs with Lines
2710 West 47th Avenue
Spokane, Washington 99224
Phone: (509) 747-0315
Fax: (509) 624-0383
E-mail: homestitches@gmetch.net
Web site: www.homestitches.com

Frankie Schmitt
Dizzy Stitches
18806 73rd Avenue NE
Kenmore, Washington 98028
Phone: (425) 485-5859
E-mail: dizzy@oz.net

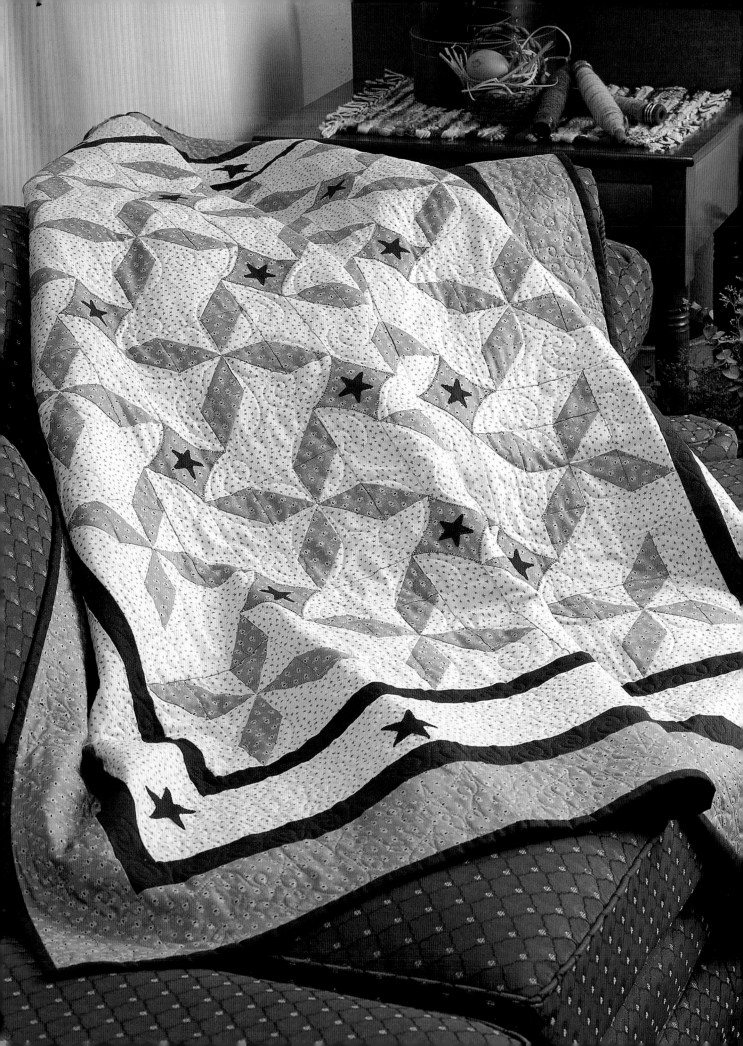

About the Authors

Retta Warehime (left)
Beth Merrill Kovich (right)

BETH MERRILL KOVICH started sewing when her maternal great-grandmother presented her with a toy hand-crank Singer sewing machine on her third birthday. Her mother, Molly Merrill, is responsible for nurturing her love of quilting, and they enjoy collaborating whenever they can. For some people, fabric is the inspiration behind their projects, but for Beth it is the quilters in her life, past and present, who kindle her passion for quilting.

Beth has contributed designs and quilts to several Martingale & Company books. Sharing her enthusiasm for quilting is a priority, and she loves teaching quilting classes. She is currently adding "motherhood" to her roster and looking forward to lots of baby projects. Beth resides in Woodinville, Washington, with her husband, Tom, and their ever-growing houseful of hobbies.

RETTA WAREHIME has been quilting and designing for over 20 years now. She is currently employed at Fiber Mosaics, where she is the quilt designer and editor-in-chief. Retta's company Sew Cherished is still very active. "When I leave work each night, the ideas just keep coming. I don't do much sewing at Fiber Mosaics anymore, so my outlet is coming home and sewing my own designs—thanks to Martingale. This year I decided to start giving away my work. My goal is to have each good friend and relative receive an original quilt that was designed by me. Three of the quilts from this book are already given away. It is so easy and fun to share."

Retta has resided in Kennewick, Washington, for over thirteen years now, and Spokane, Washington, prior to that. Her house is full with two kids still living at home, two grown-up kids that are in and out, two grand-kids, and two hockey players that live there eight months out of the year. As Retta says, "Life is good."

new and bestselling titles from

America's Best-Loved Craft & Hobby Books®

That Patchwork Place®

America's Best-Loved Quilt Books®

NEW RELEASES
1000 Great Quilt Blocks
Basically Brilliant Knits
Bright Quilts from Down Under
Christmas Delights
Creative Machine Stitching
Crochet for Tots
Crocheted Aran Sweaters
Cutting Corners
Everyday Embellishments
Folk Art Friends
Garden Party
Hocus Pocus!
Just Can't Cut It!
Quilter's Home: Winter, The
Sweet and Simple Baby Quilts
Time to Quilt
Today's Crochet
Traditional Quilts to Paper Piece

APPLIQUÉ
Appliquilt in the Cabin
Artful Album Quilts
Artful Appliqué
Blossoms in Winter
Color-Blend Appliqué
Sunbonnet Sue All through the Year

BABY QUILTS
Easy Paper-Pieced Baby Quilts
Even More Quilts for Baby
More Quilts for Baby
Play Quilts
Quilted Nursery, The
Quilts for Baby

HOLIDAY QUILTS & CRAFTS
Christmas Cats and Dogs
Creepy Crafty Halloween
Handcrafted Christmas, A
Make Room for Christmas Quilts
Welcome to the North Pole

HOME DECORATING
Decorated Kitchen, The
Decorated Porch, The
Dresden Fan
Gracing the Table
Make Room for Quilts
Quilts for Mantels and More
Sweet Dreams

LEARNING TO QUILT
101 Fabulous Rotary-Cut Quilts
Beyond the Blocks
Casual Quilter, The
Feathers That Fly
Joy of Quilting, The
Simple Joys of Quilting, The
Your First Quilt Book (or it should be!)

PAPER PIECING
40 Bright and Bold Paper-Pieced Blocks
50 Fabulous Paper-Pieced Stars
For the Birds
Quilter's Ark, A

TOPICS IN QUILTMAKING
American Stenciled Quilts
Americana Quilts
Batik Beauties
Bed and Breakfast Quilts
Fabulous Quilts from Favorite Patterns
Frayed-Edge Fun
Patriotic Little Quilts
Reversible Quilts

CRAFTS
ABCs of Making Teddy Bears, The
Blissful Bath, The
Handcrafted Frames
Handcrafted Garden Accents
Handprint Quilts
Painted Chairs
Painted Whimsies

KNITTING & CROCHET
365 Knitting Stitches a Year Perpetual
  Calendar
Clever Knits
Crochet for Babies and Toddlers
Crocheted Sweaters
Knitted Sweaters for Every Season
Knitted Throws and More
Knitter's Book of Finishing Techniques, The
Knitter's Template, A
More Paintbox Knits
Paintbox Knits
Too Cute! Cotton Knits for Toddlers
Treasury of Rowan Knits, A
Ultimate Knitter's Guide, The

...d your favorite craft, fabric, and yarn
... you're looking for, visit us at
...m or contact us at:

...-3126

...25-483-3313

...36-7596

...gale-pub.com

... of our titles, visit our Web site.

1/03